The Snowman's Song
A Christmas Story

illustrations by Tracy La Rue Hohn
story by Marilee Joy Mayfield

There is not enough darkness in the world
to extinguish the light of one small candle.
Spanish proverb

Leaping Antelope Productions® books are available for sales promotions, premiums and fund-raising use. Special editions can also be created to specification. For details, contact the publishers at Leaping Antelope Productions, 1-888-909-LEAP, www.leapingantelope.com.

Illustrations by Tracy La Rue Hohn
www.larueoriginals.com

ISBN 13: 978-0-9762059-5-1
ISBN 10: 0-9762059-5-5

It's true, you know,
that people of snow
send their thoughts around
without making a sound.

"I want to sing!"
The little snowman
sent this thought to his mother.
"I want to have a heavenly voice.
It's Christmastime, I want to rejoice!"

"I'm sorry, my son, you don't have a choice.
A child of snow doesn't have a voice."

But her little son snowman
had so many strong wishes
he wanted to share
that he made a windstorm
of whirling thought air.

The cardinal's voice was so sweet and clear
he almost felt he had ears to hear.
"Why can't I sing like you?"
thought the little snowman.

"Of course you can...
but before you can change who you are
hold hope in your heart
and look for a star."

So the sad little snowman put on a brave face.
He worked hard to replace
his doubts and his fears
with thoughts of sweet songs,
music, bells ringing, and choirs.

Deep in his soul like a warm, glowing fire
his bright wish remained, his one heart's desire.
Each day was a chance to make a new start,
but by night he cried ice and felt cold in his heart.

Sometimes he looked up
for signs in the sky.
But nothing was happening.
He couldn't make sounds.

Despite all his wishing,
no one seemed aware
that deep in the park,
in the snow, he was there.

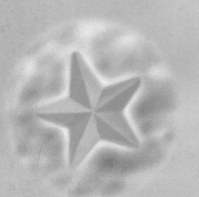

But one day he woke up
and something was new.
The morning was crisp,
the sky was bright blue.

He felt powdery footsteps...
"Mommy, look what I found!"
A small girl stood near him,
then she jumped up and down.

For most of the day, she played beside him.
She straightened his hat
and turned up its brim.
She draped her red winter scarf
around his round middle.
She sang him three songs
and she told him a riddle.
Then she dangled her store-bought
glass beads and charms
all over his long carrot nose and both arms.

"Let's go home," said her mom.
We'll come back to play another day."

But the little girl didn't want to go home.
Her once joyful thoughts took a more somber tone.
She ran up to the side of his sad snowy face
and whispered these words, which felt like an embrace.
"I hear your music even though you can't speak."
And then she leaned over and kissed his cold cheek.

He wanted so much to sing just one small note.
But nothing would come from
his cold, hard snow throat.
But something was happening…
he just didn't know
for where she had kissed him
she left a warm glow.
So the snow melted slightly inside of his face
and the hint of a smile had appeared, just a trace.

The night before Christmas
was the worst night he'd had.
All around there was music.
Everyone seemed so glad.

He silently stood in his place in the park.
His feelings were frozen, his thoughts were so dark.
His mother was worried, she felt his despair
and she tried to send comfort to him through the air.

He knew that she cared.
But his cold heavy silence was too sad to be shared.
He bowed his head and shut his eyes tight.
Snow was starting to fall, it was such a cold night.
With the last ounce of courage that only faith brings
his thoughts formed this prayer with frost-covered wings.

"Please let me sing a song filled with light.
Then my life will be perfect, my thoughts will be right.
And all the sweet sounds angels use to stop doubt
will burst forth from my heart and out of my mouth
like a powdery snow over this holy night."

He almost missed her soft steps in the snow.
She was holding a candle that gave a warm glow.

'Round his neck there was tinkling,
like spoons hitting glass.
She had made him a necklace
in her second grade class.
Silver bells, gold stars,
and snowflakes of blue,
it was beautifully fashioned
and it made music, too.

Then the winter wind came
with a huge, forceful blast.
The tinkling bell necklace swirled 'round very fast.
And all of a sudden his mouth opened wide
and heavenly music flew out from inside.

His song was spring rains and violin strings,
the fragrance of flowers and hummingbird wings,
words of great kindness, the faith in our hymns,
the shine in our eyes and a little girl's whims.
More joyful than angels, more peaceful than sleep,
filled with longing and prayers and memories to keep.

She knew he had heard her.
It was golden and true.
The wonder of Christmas
surrounded these two.